THE AUTHORS

Luca Stefano Cristini has edited various publications on ancient and contemporary historical themes, including books on thirty years war, Medieval, Napoleonic as well as several illustrated books with historical color photographs. He has also curated all the brands of Soldiershop publishing.

Joel Bellviure is a young Spanish historical researcher. He is particularly interested in early color photography techniques, colourisation, and History. He is currently studying History at the University of Barcelona. He is also the creator of Cassowary Colorizations.

PUBLISHING'S NOTES

LICENSES COMMONS

ACKNOWLEDGEMENTS

A Special Thanks to Doug, Richard, Anthony, Toussaint , Rui and Jan Meyer. Thanks to the Europeana Collections, and at all the several institution, museum, library, bibliotecks, public or private collection & athenaeums that with their positive copyright policy about part of his collections, allows us the use of many images present in our books. We remember same of this great World Institutions: New York Public Library, Rara CH, Heidelberg Biblioteck University, US Library of Congress, Riikmuseum of Amsterdam, Dusseldorf University Library, Polona Library, Herzog August Bibliothek of Wolfenbüttel, Stuttgart Bibliothek, SLUB Dresden, Frankfurt am Main Universitätsbibliothek, Europeana, Wikipedia, and many others...

To my friends of Berliner Zinnfiguren..!

Title: **GERMAN & FRENCH ARMIES IN THE GREAT WAR** - Soldati tedeschi e francesi nella Grande Guerra
By Luca Stefano Cristini e Joel Bellviure.
ISBN code: 978-88-93273022 First edition January 2018
Code.: **WW1-004,**

Cover & Art Design: Luca S. Cristini
WW1&2 brand is a trademark of Soldiershop Publishing, via Padre Davide, 7 - 24050 Zanica (BG) ITALY.

GERMAN & FRENCH ARMIES IN THE GREAT WAR

1914-1918 SOLDATI TEDESCHI E FRANCESI NELLA GRANDE GUERRA

BY LUCA STEFANO CRISTINI & JOEL BELLVIURE

BOOKS TO COLLECT

THE GREAT WAR IN COLOUR

EXTRAORDINARY COLOURISED IMAGES BRING TO LIFE THE HORRORS FACING ALL THE SOLDIERS DURING THE FIRST WORLD WAR

When you look at old black and white photos, the past seems very far away. This is especially apparent with First World War photographs. Soldiershop is proud to present in the 100th anniversary of the end of the First World War his project of colorized images of the WW1, The images featured not only the great battles of the war, but also life on the home front, wartime industries, the hospitals, the advances in the field of technology and communications ...

The Great War in Colour project will consist of colourizing of several of the better images about the year 1914-1918 from various Library and Archives of the world.

A Special Thanks to the several institution, museum, library, bibliotecks, public or private collection & athenaeums that with their positive copyright policy about part of his collections, allows us the use of many images present in our books realized for the centennial of the Armistice.

Several million black-and-white photos exist in the world's archives of events during the First World War, captured in myriad photographs on all sides of the front. Most of this photos show the devastating events of the Great War were.

Since then, a lot of books of black-and-white photographs of the war have been published as all nations endeavour to comprehend the scale and the carnage of the "terrible war of the 20th century". To mark the centenary of the outbreak of war, our books brings together all of these remarkable, fully recolored images of WW1.

The volume represents the work of several artists and collaborators of Soldiershop, but especially it is based on the work of the two main authors: Luca Cristini and Joel Bellviure.

Our book presents all the text of the plates in English and Italian language.

◄ 1915, a studio photograph of a fully-equipped young Imperial German soldier with a Gewehr 98 and a trench flashlight, c. 1915. The flowers tucked into his uniform were an indication that he would be sent to the frontline very soon.

1915, Un giovanissimo e ben armato soldato tedesco, col fiore nella cinta ad indicare un veloce rientro a casa.

LA GRANDE GUERRA A COLORI

STRAORDINARIE IMMAGINI RICOLORATE RIDANNO VITA AGLI ORRORI PATITI DA TUTTI I SOLDATI DURANTE LA PRIMA GUERRA MONDIALE

Quando si guardano le vecchie foto in bianco e nero, il passato sembra molto lontano. Questo è particolarmente evidente soprattutto con le fotografie della prima guerra mondiale. Soldiershop, nel centenario della Grande Guerra vi offre una biblioteca unica e innovativa con questa serie di foto colorate della prima guerra mondiale.

Le immagini non trattano solo le importanti battaglie della guerra, ma anche la vita sul fronte domestico, le industrie, gli ospedali, i progressi della tecnica e delle comunicazioni...

Il progetto "Great war in colour" consiste nella accurata selezione e poi ricolorazione di alcune delle migliori immagini relative agli anni 1914-1918 provenienti da varie biblioteche e archivi del mondo.

Il nostro ringraziamento speciale va a tutte quelle diverse istituzioni, musei, biblioteche, collezioni pubbliche o private e atenei che con la loro politica aperta in materia di copyright relativa all'uso di parte delle loro collezioni ci hanno permesso l'uso di molte immagini presenti nei nostri libri realizzati specificatamente per il centenario dell'armistizio.

Diversi milioni di foto in bianco e nero esistono negli archivi mondiali di eventi relativi alla prima guerra mondiale, una miriade di "scatti" raccolti su tutti i lati del fronte, per lo più da fotografi rimasti anonimi. La maggior parte di queste foto mostrano gli eventi devastanti della Grande Guerra, ma anche la vita di tutti i giorni nelle trincee e nelle linee di prossimità e nelle retrovie. Ed ancora negli ospedali, nelle cucine nelle fabbriche impegnate nello sforzo bellico.

Da allora, sono stati pubblicati moltissimi libri di fotografie in bianco e nero della guerra, in quanto tutte le nazioni, coinvolte e no, si sono sforzate di comprendere la scala, la carneficina e tutte le terribile complicazioni provocate dalla "terribile guerra del XX secolo".

Per celebrare il centenario dello scoppio della guerra, i nostri libri riuniscono tutte queste straordinarie e ricolorate immagini della WW1.

Il volume rappresenta l'opera di diversi artisti e collaboratori di Soldiershop, ma si basa soprattutto sul lavoro dei due principali autori: Luca Cristini e Joel Bellviure.

I libri della serie WW1 presentano tutto il testo e le note didascaliche in lingua inglese e italiana.

◀ Two cheerful soldiers from the 43th Infantry Regiment during the Battle of the Somme, September 1916.
Due soldati francesi del 43° Reggimento di fanteria. Battaglia delle Somme, Settembre 1916.

THE IMPERIAL GERMAN ARMY

DEUTSCHES HEER

IMPERIAL GERMAN ARMY

The **Imperial German Army** (*Deutsches Heer*) was the name given to the combined land and air forces of the German Empire (excluding the *Marine-Fliegerabteilung* maritime aviation formations of the *Kaiserliche Marine*).

FORMATION OF THE ARMY

The states that made up the German Empire contributed their armies; within the German Confederation, formed after the Napoleonic Wars, each state was responsible for maintaining certain units to be put at the disposal of the Confederation in case of conflict. When operating together, the units were known as the Federal Army (*Bundesheer*). Prussia formed the North German Confederation and the treaty provided for the maintenance of a Federal Army and a Federal Navy (*Bundesmarine* or *Bundeskriegsmarine*). Further laws on military duty also used these terms. Conventions were entered into between the North German Confederation and its member states, subordinating their armies to the Prussian army in time of war, and giving the Prussian Army control over training, doctrine and equipment. After 1871, the peacetime armies of the four kingdoms remained relatively distinct. "German Army" was used in various legal documents, such as the Military Penal Code, but otherwise the Prussian, Bavarian, Saxon and Württemberg armies maintained distinct identities. Each kingdom had its own War Ministry, Bavaria and Saxony published their own rank and seniority lists for their officers and the Württemberg list was a separate chapter of the Prussian army rank lists. Württemberg and Saxon units were numbered according to the Prussian system but Bavarian units maintained their own numbers (the 2nd Württemberg Infantry Regiment was Infantry Regiment No. 120 under the Prussian system).

COMMAND

The commander of the Imperial German Army, less the Bavarian contingent, was the Kaiser. He was assisted by a Military Cabinet and exercised control through the Prussian Ministry of War and the Great General Staff. The Chief of the General Staff became the Kaiser's main military advisor and the most powerful military figure in the Empire. Bavaria kept its own Ministry of War and General Staff, but coordinated planning with the Prussian Great General Staff. Saxony also maintained its own Ministry of War and the Ministry of War of Württemberg also continued to exist. Command of the Prussian Army had been reformed in the wake of the defeats suffered by Prussia in the Napoleonic Wars. Rather than rely primarily on the martial skills of the individual members of the German nobility, who dominated the military profession, the Prussian Army instituted changes to ensure excellence in leadership, organization and planning. The General Staff system, that sought to institutionalize military excellence, was the main result. It sought to identify military talent at the lower levels and develop it thoroughly through academic training and practical experience on division, corps and higher staffs, up to the Great General Staff, the senior planning body of the army. It provided planning and organizational work during peacetime and wartime. The Prussian General Staff, proven in battle in the Wars of Unification, became the German General Staff upon formation of the German Empire, given Prussia's leading role in the German Army.

◄ Young German *Stoßtruppen* (Schock trooper) during the Battle of the Somme, late 1916.
Due giovani fratelli tedeschi in posa per la partenza al fronte del più vecchio dei due. Agosto 1914

Chiefs of the German General Staff in WW1
- Helmuth von Moltke the Younger 1 January 1906 – 14 September 1914
- Erich von Falkenhayn 14 September 1914 – 29 August 1916
- Paul von Hindenburg 29 August 1916 – 3 July 1919
- Wilhelm Groener 3 July 1919 – 7 July 1919
- Hans von Seeckt 7 July 1919 – 15 July 1919

STRUCTURE

The basic peacetime organizational structure of the Imperial German Army were the Army inspectorate (*Armee-Inspektion*), the army corps (*Armeekorps*), the division and the regiment. During wartime, the staff of the Army inspectorates formed field army commands, which controlled the corps and subordinate units. During World War I, a higher command level, the army group (*Heeresgruppe*), was created. Each army group controlled several field armies.

CORPS (*ARMEEKORPS*)

The basic organizational formation was the army corps (*Armeekorps*). The corps consisted of two or more divisions and various support troops, covering a geographical area. The corps was also responsible for maintaining the reserves and *Landwehr* in the corps area. By 1914, there were 21 corps areas under Prussian jurisdiction and three Bavarian army corps. Besides the regional corps, there was also a Guard Corps (*Gardecorps*), which controlled the elite Prussian Guard units. A corps usually included a light infantry (Jäger) battalion, a heavy artillery (*Fußartillerie*) battalion, an engineer battalion, a telegraph battalion and a trains battalion. Some corps areas also disposed of fortress troops; each of the 25 corps had a Field Aviation Unit (*Feldflieger Abteilung*) attached to it normally equipped with six unarmed "A" or "B" class unarmed two-seat observation aircraft apiece.

In wartime, the army corps became a mobile tactical formation and four *Höhere Kavallerie-Kommando* (Higher Cavalry Commands) were formed from the Cavalry Inspectorate, the equivalent of corps, being made up of two divisions of cavalry.

The areas formerly covered by the corps each became the responsibility of a *Wehrkreis* (Military District, sometimes translated as Corps Area). The Military Districts were to supervise the training and enlistment of reservists and new recruits. Originally each Military District was linked to an army corps; thus Wehrkreis I took over the area that I. Armeekorps had been responsible for and sent replacements to the same formation. The first sixteen Reserve Corps raised followed the same pattern; X. Reserve-Korps was made up of reservists from the same area as X. Armeekorps. However, these links between rear areas and front line units were broken as the war went on and later corps were raised with troops from all over Germany.

DIVISION

The basic tactical formation was the division. A standard Imperial German division consisted of two infantry brigades of two regiments each, a cavalry brigade of two regiments, and an artillery brigade of two regiments. One of the divisions in a corps area usually also managed the corps *Landwehr* region (*Landwehrbezirk*). In 1914, besides the Guard Corps (two Guard divisions and a Guard cavalry division), there were 42 regular divisions in the Prussian Army (including four Saxon divisions and two Württemberg divisions), and six divisions in the Bavarian Army.

These divisions were all mobilized in August 1914. They were reorganized, receiving engineer companies and other support units from their corps, and giving up most of their cavalry to form cavalry divisions. Reserve divisions were also formed, *Landwehr* brigades were aggregated into divisions, and other divisions were formed from replacement (*Ersatz*) units. As World War I progressed, additional divisions were formed, and by wars' end, 251 divisions had been formed or reformed in the German Army's structure.

REGIMENT

The regiment was the basic combat unit as well as the recruiting base for soldiers. When inducted, a soldier entered a regiment, usually through its replacement battalion, and received his basic training. There were three basic types of regiment: infantry, cavalry and artillery. Other specialties, such as pioneers (combat engineers) and signal troops, were organized into smaller support units. Regiments also carried the traditions of the army, in many cases stretching back into the 17th and 18th centuries. After World War I, regimental traditions were carried forward in the *Reichswehr* and its successor, the *Wehrmacht*, but the chain of tradition was broken in 1945 as West German and East German units did not carry forward pre-1945 traditions.

INDUSTRIAL BASE

Germany had the largest industrial base in Europe, having surpassed Britain by 1900. The Army closely cooperated with industry, especially in the World War, with particular focus on the very rapidly changing aircraft industry. The Army set prices and labor exemptions, regulated the supply of credit and raw materials, limited patent rights so as to allow cross-licensing among firms, and supervised management–labor relationships. The result was very rapid expansion and a high output of high quality aircraft, as well as high wages that attracted the best machinists. Apart from aircraft, the Army's regulation of the rest of the war economy was inefficient.

AIR FORCE

The *Deutsche Luftstreitkräfte*, known before October 1916 as *Die Fliegertruppen des deutschen Kaiserreiches* (Imperial German Flying Troops),[10] was the over-land air arm of the German Army during World War I (1914–1918). Although its name actually means something very close to "The German Air Force", it remained an integral part of the German Army for the duration of the war. The *Kaiserliche Marine* naval forces of the German Empire had their own, separate *Marine-Fliegerabteilung* maritime aviation forces, apart from the *Luftstreitkräfte* of the Army.

RANKS OF THE IMPERIAL GERMAN ARMY

The German Army from 1871 to 1914 inherited the various traditions and military ranks of its constituent states, thus becoming a truly federal armed service.

Enlisted (*Mannschaften/Gemeine*) ranks

- Musketeer (*Musketier*, Prussian army infantry regiments), Infantryman (*Infanterist*, Bavarian army infantry regiments), Soldier (*Soldat*, Saxon army infantry regiments), Gunner (*Kanonier*, foot artillery), Pioneer (*Pionier*, pioneer branch). Other unit-specific enlisted ranks were: Fusilier (*Füsilier*), Grenadier (*Grenadier*), Huntsman otherwise Light-Infantryman (*Jäger*), Dragoon (*Dragoner*), Hussar (*Husar*), Cuirassier (*Kürassier*), Uhlan (*Ulan*), Fusilier Guard (*Garde-Füsilier*), Grenadier Guard (*Garde-Grenadier*), etc.
- Lance Corporal (*Gefreiter*); up until 1918 the only rank (with exception of *Obergefreiter* in the foot artillery) to which an enlisted soldier could be promoted, the rank was a deputy rank to the Corporal (*Unteroffizier*)[11] rank.[12]
- Senior Lance Corporal (*Obergefreiter*); established in the Prussian Army from 1846 to 1853, reestablished in 1859, then in foot artillery only, replacing the artillery Bombardier rank that had been introduced in 1730.

Additionally, the following *voluntary* enlistees were distinguished:

- One-Year Volunteer Enlistee (*Einjährig-Freiwilliger*): despite the name, one-year volunteers were actually conscripts who served a short-term form of active military service, open for enlistees up to the age of 25.
- Long-Term Volunteer Enlistee "Capitulant" (*Kapitulant*): enlisted soldiers who had already absolved

·   their regular two or three-year military conscription term and had now *volunteered* to continue serving for further terms, minimum was 4 years, generally up to 12 years.

Note: *Einjährig-Freiwilliger* and *Kapitulant* were not ranks as such during this specific period of use, but *voluntary* military enlistee designations. They, however, wore a specific uniform distinction (twisted wool piping along their shoulder epaulette edging for *Einjährig-Freiwilliger*, the *Kapitulant* a narrow band across their lower shoulder epaulette) in the colours of their respective nation state. This distinction was never removed throughout their military service nor during any rank grade advancements.

Non-commissioned officers / *Unteroffiziere*

Junior NCOs (NCOs without Sword Knot) / *Unteroffizier ohne Portepee*

·   Corporal/Sub-Officer (*Unteroffizier*)
·   Sergeant

Senior NCOs (NCOs with Sword Knot) / *Unteroffizier mit Portepee*

·   Sergeant Major 2nd class (Infantry: Vice-Feldwebel, Cavalry and Artillery: Vizewachtmeister/Vice-Wachtmeister) – rank held by reserve officer candidates after they passed lieutenant's examination
·   Sergeant-Major (Infantry: Feldwebel (i.e. *Etatmäßiger Feldwebel*: CSM officially listed on the regiment's payroll, i.e. *Etat*), Cavalry and Artillery: (*Etatmäßiger*) Wachtmeister)

Warrant Officers and Officer Cadets

·   Cadet (*Fahnenjunker*, ranking between Sergeant and Vizefeldwebel) – served as cadets in the various military academies and schools.
·   Ensign (*Fähnrich*, ranking between *Vize-Feldwebel* and *Etatmäßiger Feldwebel*)
·   Deputy Officer (*Offizierstellvertreter*, ranking above *Etatmäßiger Feldwebel*)
·   Acting Lieutenant (*Feldwebelleutnant*, ranking as youngest 2nd Lieutenant, but without officer's commission and still member of the NCO's Mess until 1917)

Officer corps

Critics long believed that the Army's officer corps was heavily dominated by Junker aristocrats, so that commoners were shunted into low-prestige branches, such as the heavy artillery or supply. However, by the 1890s, the top ranks were opened to highly talented commoners.[17][18]

Subalterns / *Subalternoffiziere*

·   2nd Lieutenant (*Leutnant* in the infantry, cavalry and other arms, *Feuerwerksleutnant* in the artillery)
·   First Lieutenant (*Oberleutnant*, *Feuerwerksoberleutnant*)
·   Staff Captain (Infantry and Artillery: *Hauptmann/Kapitän II Klasse*, Cavalry: *Rittmeister II Klasse*)
·   Captain (Infantry and Artillery: *Hauptmann/Kapitän I Klasse*, Cavalry: *Rittmeister I Klasse*)

Staff Officers / *Stabsoffiziere*

·   Major
·   Lieutenant Colonel (*Oberstleutnant*)
·   Colonel (*Oberst*)

General Officers / *Generäle*

·   Major General (*Generalmajor*)
·   Lieutenant General (*Generalleutnant*)
·   General of the Infantry, General of the Cavalry, General of the Artillery (*General der Infanterie, General der Kavallerie, General der Artillerie*)
·   Colonel General (*Generaloberst*)
·   Colonel General in the rank of General Field Marshal (*Generaloberst mit dem Rang als Generalfeldmarschall*)
·   General Field Marshal (*Generalfeldmarschall*)

THE FRENCH ARMY

ARMÉE FRANÇAISE

FRENCH ARMY IN WORLD WAR I

During World War I, France was one of the Triple Entente powers allied against the Central Powers. Although fighting occurred worldwide, the bulk of the fighting in Europe occurred in Belgium, Luxembourg, France and Alsace-Lorraine along what came to be known as the Western Front, which consisted mainly of trench warfare. Specific operational, tactical, and strategic decisions by the high command on both sides of the conflict led to shifts in organizational capacity, as the French Army tried to respond to day-to-day fighting and long-term strategic and operational agendas. In particular, many problems caused the French high command to re-evaluate standard procedures, revise its command structures, re-equip the army, and to develop different tactical approaches.

BACKGROUND

France had been the major power in Europe for most of the Early Modern Era. After 1870, the European powers began gaining settlements in Africa, with colonialism on that continent hitting its peak between 1895 and 1905. However, colonial disputes were only a minor cause of World War I, as most had been settled by 1914. Economic rivalry was not only a source for some of the colonial conflicts but also a minor cause for the start of World War I. For France the rivalry was mostly with the rapidly industrializing Germany, which had seized the coal-rich region of Alsace-Lorraine in 1870, and later struggled with France over mineral-rich Morocco. Another cause of World War I was growing militarism which led to an arms race between the powers. As a result of the arms race, all European powers were ready for war. France was bound by treaty to defend Russia. Austria–Hungary had declared war on Serbia due to the Black Hand's assassination of Archduke Ferdinand, which acted as the immediate cause of the war. France was brought into the war by a German declaration of war on August 3, 1914.

THE PRE-WAR ARMY AND MOBILIZATION

In common with most other continental European powers, the French Army was organised on the basis of universal conscription. Each year, the "class" of men turning twenty-one in the upcoming year would be inducted into the French Army and spend three years in active service. After leaving active service they would progress through various stages of reserves, each of which involved a lower degree of commitment.

- Active Army (20–23)
- Reserve of the Active Army (24–34)
- Territorial Army (35–41)
- Reserve of the Territorial Army (42–48)

The peacetime army consisted of 173 infantry regiments, 89 cavalry regiments and 87 artillery regiments. All were substantially under strength and would be filled out on mobilisation by the first three classes of the Reserve (that is, men between 24 and 26). Each regiment would also leave behind a cadre of training personnel to conduct refresher courses for the older reservists, who were organized into 201 Reserve Regiments and 145 Territorial Regiments. Above the regimental level, France was divided into 22 Military Regions, each of which would become a Army Corps on mobilisation.

At the apex of the French Army was the General Staff, since 1911 under the leadership of General Joseph Joffre. The General Staff was responsible for drawing up the plan for mobilisation, known as Plan XVII. Using the railroad network, the Army would be shifted from their peacetime garrisons throughout France to the eastern border with Germany. The order for mobilisation was given on 1 August, the same day that Germany declared war on Russia.

ORGANIZATION DURING THE WAR

Upon mobilization, Joffre became Commander-in-Chief of the French Army. Most of his forces were concentrated in the north east of France, both to attack Alsace-Lorraine and to meet the expected German offensive through the Low Countries.

- First Army (7th, 8th, 13th, 14th, and 21st Army Corps), with the objective of capturing Mulhouse.
- Second Army (9th, 15th, 16th, 18th and 20th Army Corps), with the objective of capturing Morhange.
- Third Army (4th, 5th and 6th Army Corps), defending the region around Metz.
- Fourth Army (12th, 17th and Colonial Army Corps) held in reserve around the Forest of Argonne
- Fifth Army (1st, 2nd, 3rd, 10th and 11th Army Corps), defending the Ardennes.

Over the course of the First World War another five field armies would be raised. The war scare led to another 2.9 million men being mobilized in the summer of 1914 and the costly battles on the Western Front forced France to conscript men up to the age of 45. This was done by the mobilization in 1914 of the Territorial Army and its reserves; comprising men who had completed their peacetime service with the active and reserve armies (ages 20–34). In June 1915, the Allied countries met in the first inter-Allied conference Britain, France, Belgium, Italy, Serbia and Russia agreed to coordinate their attacks but the attempts were frustrated by German offensives on the Eastern Front and spoiling offensives at Ypres and in the hills west of Verdun. By 1918, towards the end of the war, the composition and structure of the French army had changed. Forty percent of all French soldiers on the Western Front were operating artillery and 850,000 French troops were infantry in 1918, compared to 1.5 million in 1915. Causes for the drop in infantry include increased machine gun, armored car and tank usage, as well as the increasing significance of the French air force, the Service Aéronautique. At the end of the war on November 11, 1918, the French had called up 8,317,000 men, including 475,000 colonial troops. France suffered over 4.2 million casualties, with 1.3 million dead.

COMMANDERS IN CHIEF

Joseph Joffre was Commander-in-Chief, a position for which he had been designated since 1911. While serving in this position, Joffre was responsible for development of the Plan XVII the mobilisation and concentration plan for the offensive strategy against Germany, which proved a costly failure.

Joffre was thought to be the 'Savior of France' due to his serenity and a refusal to admit defeat, valuable at the beginning of the war, along with his regrouping of retreating Allied forces at the Battle of the Marne. Joffre was effectively relieved of his duties on December 13, 1916, following the heavy human losses at the Battle of Verdun and the Somme, and the defeat of Romania, which appeared for a time to put the Salonika Bridgehead in jeopardy. Due to his popularity, it was not presented to the public as a dismissal when he was promoted to Marshal of France on the same day.

Robert Nivelle, who began the war as a regimental colonel, was appointed Commander-in-Chief. However, after the failure of the Nivelle Offensive in April 1917 he was removed from his position and appointed Commander-in-Chief in North Africa.

On May 15, 1917, Philippe Pétain was made Commander-in-Chief after a few weeks as Army Chief of Staff. The French Army Mutinies had begun during that period, and he restored the fighting capability of the French troops by improving front line living conditions, and conducting only limited offensives. In the Third Battle of the Aisne, fought in May 1918, French positions collapsed due to the local commander General Duchene's defiance of Pétain's recommendation of defence in depth, and Petain's pessimism saw him subordinated to the Supreme Allied Commander Ferdinand Foch.

WESTERN FRONT

Germany marched through neutral Belgium as part of the Schlieffen Plan to invade France, and by August 23 had reached the French border town of Maubeuge, whose true significance lay within its forts. Maubeuge was a major railway junction and was consequently a protected city. It had 15 forts and gun batteries, totaling 435 guns, along with a permanent garrison of 35,000 troops, a number enhanced by the British Expeditionary Force. The BEF and the French Fifth Army retreated on August 23, and the town was besieged by German heavy artillery starting on August 25. The fortress was surrendered on September 7 by General Fournier, who was later court-martialed, but exonerated, for the capitulation.

The Battle of Guise, launched on August 29, was an attempt by the Fifth Army to capture Guise, they succeeded, but later withdrew on August 30. This delayed the German Second Army's invasion of France, but also hurt Lanrezac's already damaged reputation. The First Battle of the Marne was fought between September 6 and September 12. It started when retreating French forces (the Fifth and Sixth armies), stopped south of the Marne River. Victory seemed close, the First German Army was given orders to surround Paris, unaware the French government had already fled to Bordeaux. The First Battle of the Marne was a French victory, but was a bloody one: the French suffered 250,000 casualties, of which 80,000 died, with similar numbers believed for the Germans, and over 12,700 for the British.The German retreat after the First Battle of the Marne halted at the Aisne River, and the Allies soon caught up, starting the First Battle of the Aisne on September 12. It lasted until September 28, it was indecisive, partially due to machine guns beating back infantry sent to capture enemy positions. In the Battle of Le Cateau, fought on August 26–27, the French Sixth Army prevented the British from being outflanked. The first major Allied attack against German forces since the incarnation of trench warfare on the Western Front, the First Battle of Champagne, lasting from December 20, 1914, until March 17, 1915; it was a German victory, due in part to their machine gun battalions and the well-entrenched German forces.

The indecisive Second Battle of Ypres, from April 22 – May 25, was the site of the first German chlorine gas attack and the only major German offensive on the Western Front in 1915. Ypres was devastated after the battle. The Second Battle of Artois, from May 9 – June 18, the most important part of the Allied spring offensive of 1915, was successful for the Germans, allowing them to advance rather than retreat as the Allies had planned, and Artois would not be in Allied hands again until 1917. The Second Battle of Champagne, from September 25 – November 6, was a general failure, with the French only advancing about 4 kilometres (2.5 mi), and not capturing the German's second line. France suffered over 140,000 casualties, while the Germans suffered over 80,000.

The Battle of the Somme, fought along a 30 kilometres (19 mi) front from north of the Somme River between Arras and Albert. It was fought between July 1 and November 18 and involved over 2 million men. The French suffered 200,000 casualties. Little territory was gained, only 12 kilometres (7.5 mi) at the deepest points.

EQUIPMENT

At the outset of the war, the primary French field gun was the French 75, (75mm caliber, entered service in 1897). The French had about 4,000 of these guns, an adequate number, but despite accuracy, quick firing, and lethality against infantry, German howitzers outranged the French 75, which had a range of 7 kilometres (4.3 mi), by 3 kilometres (1.9 mi), and used heavier shells, inflicting more damage than the French guns. In 1913, General Joseph Joffre authorized the limited adoption of the Rimailho Model 1904TR, a howitzer with a range of over 10 kilometres (6.2 mi).

When war broke out in August 1914, the German Army had about 12,000 machine guns, while the British and French armies had a few hundred. French models of machine gun used during the war included the

Hotchkiss M1914, the Chauchat, and the St. Étienne Mle 1907.

The first tank was ready for combat by January 1916. Unaware of the British tank development programme, Colonel Jean Baptiste Eugène Estienne persuaded Joffre to begin production of French tanks. An order for 400 Schneider CA1s and 400 Saint-Chamonds was soon placed. The French deployed 128 tanks in April 1917 as part of the Second Battle of the Aisne, but they were unreliable. However, the Renault FT proved more worthy, and the French produced a total of 3,870 tanks by the end of the war.

Grenades came to the attention of German military planners as a result of the Russo-Japanese war of 1904–1905, and by the beginning of the Great War, the Germans had 106,000 rifle grenades and 70,000 hand grenades. The French and Russian armies were better prepared than the British, expecting to find themselves besieging German fortresses, a task suited to the grenade. The French, along with the British, persisted in the use of rifle grenades (they used a special cup for launching) throughout the war, increasing their range from 180 and 200 metres (590 and 660 ft) to 400 metres (1,300 ft). The mortar also interested the Germans, for a specific use: an invasion of France's eastern front. The advantage of a mortar was that it could be fired from the relative safety of a trench, unlike artillery. At the beginning of World War I, the German Army had a stockpile of 150 mortars, which was a surprise to the French and British. The French were able to use the century-old Coehorn mortars from the Napoleonic Wars. Subsequently, the French borrowed the design of the British Stokes Mortar, and collaborated on mortar designs with the British throughout the war. Eventually, large mortars could throw bombs 2 kilometres (1.2 mi).

Despite the technological advances in grenades, machine guns, and mortars, the rifle remained the primary infantry weapon, in large part because other weapons were too cumbersome and unwieldy for an infantryman, and remained the weapon of choice for snipers. Rifles remained virtually the same during the war years, mostly because research tended to be focused on larger weapons and poison gas. The average range of a rifle throughout World War I was 1,400 metres (4,600 ft), but most were only accurate to 600 metres (2,000 ft).

The French rifle of choice was the Lebel Model 1886, officially styled the Fusil Modèle 1886-M93, from 1886. Its major design flaw was its eight-round tubular magazine which could cause explosions when the nose of one cartridge was forced onto the base of another. In 1916, the Berthier rifle, officially titled the Fusil d'Infanterie Modele 1907, Transforme 1915, was issued as an improvement; it was clip-loaded.

The original, produced in 1907, only held three rounds. Later versions in 1915 introduced the use of spitzer bullets and 1916 increased the clip size to five rounds, and a carbine version of the Berthier, dubbed the Berthier carbine but titled Mousqueton modele 1916, was released in 1916. The carbine was preferred over a 'normal' rifle because of the advantages in handling in a confined space, such as a trench, and was one of the few significant advances in rifle technology, although periscopes and tripods were produced for trench warfare.

Contrary to popular belief, the first country to use chemical warfare in World War I was not Germany, but France, who used tear gas grenades against the German army in August 1914; however, the Germans were the first to seriously research chemical warfare. Poison gas (chlorine) was first used on April 22, 1915, at the Second Battle of Ypres, by the German army.

April 1915 saw the first innovation in protection against chemical warfare: a cotton pad dipped in bicarbonate of soda, but by 1918, troops on both sides had charcoal respirators. By November 11, 1918, France had suffered 190,000 chemical warfare casualties, including 8,000 dead.

UNIFORMS

At the outbreak of war the French Army retained the colourful traditional uniforms of the nineteenth century for active service wear. These included conspicuous features such as blue coats and red trousers for the infantry and cavalry. The French cuirassiers wore plumed helmets and breastplates almost unchanged from the Napoleonic period. From 1903 on several attempts had been made to introduce a more practical field dress but these had been opposed by conservative opinion both within the army and amongst the public at large. In particular, the red trousers worn by the infantry became a political debating point. Adolphe Messimy who was briefly Minister of War in 1911-1912 stated that "This stupid blind attachment to the most visible of colours will have cruel consequences"; however, in the following year, one of his successors, Eugène Étienne, declared "Abolish red trousers? Never!"

In order to appease traditionalists, a new cloth was devised woven from red, white and blue threads, known as "Tricolour cloth", resulting in a drab purple-brown colour. Unfortunately the red thread could only be produced with a dye made in Germany, so only the blue and white threads were used. The adoption of the blue-grey uniform (known as "horizon-blue" because it was thought to prevent soldiers from standing out against the skyline) had been approved by the French Government in June 1914 but new issues had not been possible before the outbreak of war a few weeks later.

The very heavy French losses during the Battle of the Frontiers can be attributed in part to the high visibility of the French uniforms, combined with peacetime training which placed emphasis on attacking in massed formations. The shortcomings of the uniforms were quickly realized and during the first quarter of 1915 general distribution of horizon-blue clothing in simplified patterns had been undertaken. The long established infantry practice of wearing greatcoats for field service, buttoned back when on the march, was continued in the trenches. British-style puttees were issued in place of leather gaiters from October 1914. The French Army was the first to introduce steel helmets for protection against shrapnel, and by December 1915 more than three million "Adrian" helmets had been manufactured.

The horizon-blue uniform and Adrian helmet proved sufficiently practical to be retained unchanged for the remainder of the war, although khaki of a shade described as "mustard" was introduced after December 1914 for the North African and colonial troops serving in France.

▲ Brothers in arms military postcard 1914.
Fratelli in arme, allegoria che simboleggia l'alleanza franco-britannica. 1914

THE GERMANS

I TEDESCHI

◄ 1916 August Schlenker (1891-1966), a railway worker from Schwäbisch-Hall, standing on a studio in Prussian blue uniform, along his two brothers, Willi and Otto Schlenker.

1916 Il soldato August Schlenker (1891-1966), addetto alle ferrovie militari, in una foto di studio nella sua uniforme bleu di Prussia accanto ai due suoi fratelli: Willi e Otto Schlenker.

1914 THE KAISER MEN GO TO THE WAR

1914 TUONANO I CANNONI D'AGOSTO

◄ **1915** "Smoking makes digging easier." Propaganda postcard encouraging camaraderie between different units during the war, depicting two German soldiers.

1915 "Fumare facilita lo scavo delle trincee". Cartolina propagandistica che incoraggia il cameratismo tra le diverse unità durante la guerra, qui raffigurante da due soldati tedeschi.

▼ **1913 SH foot artileery:** Richard Lauxen (in the middle) with four other volunteers from the clothing department of Schleswig-Holstein 9th Foot Artillery Regiment in Koblenz,.

1913 SH artiglieria a piedi: l'artigliere Richard Lauxen, (nel mezzo nella foto) con altri quattro volontari dello stesso dipartimento del 9° regg. Di ariglieria di Coblenza nello Schleswig-Holstein.

◄ **1914 U-boat commander Otto Weddigen** (1882-1915) with his wife. He and all aboard the submarine he commanded were killed when they were rammed by the British battleship HMS Dreadnought on 18th March

1914 Il comandante di un unità U-Boat Otto Weddigen (1882-1915) con sua moglie. Lui e tutti gli altri uomini a bordo del sottomarino che comandava rimasero vittima nell'affondamento della loro unità speronata dalla nave da guerra britannica HMS Dreadnought il 18 marzo del 1915.

▼ **1915** German officers with coats, many of them wearing the Iron Cross, outside a Fernsprecher (telephone office) in Heudicourt, Somme, France.

1915 Ufficiali tedeschi con cappotti e giacche da cavalleria, molti dei quali indossavano la Croce di ferro, fuori da un ufficio telefonico a Heudicourt, Somme, nella Francia occupata.

Czenstochau, den 10/9. 1914.

◄ **1915** Walter Janus stationed in Czestochowa during the war, was a sergeant of the first Company of the Landsturm Infantry Brigade in Glatz. His brother, the teacher Otto Janus, served as a reserve in the 38th Rifle Regiment, IX Division on the Western front. Sister Elisabeth (Liesel), enlisted as a nurse, was considered "the horror of the family". Nothing is known of their destiny.

*1915 **Walter Janus** stazionato a Czestochowa durante la guerra, era un sergente della prima Compagnia della Brigata di Fanteria di Landsturm a Glatz. Suo fratello, l'insegnante Otto Janus, ha servito come riserva nel 38° Reggimento Fucilieri, IX Divisione schierato sul fronte Ovest. La sorella Elisabeth (Liesel), arruolata come infermiera, era considerata come "l'orrore della famiglia". Non si sa nulla dl loro destino.*

▼ **1915** Three German soldiers lie dead in a trench near the Belgian border after a conflict during World War I, La Basse, France.

1915 Tre soldati tedeschi morti in una trincea prossima la confine belga nella cittadina di La Basse in Francia

◄ **1915** Franz Sinnen (1896-1916) from Jesteburg, who would eventually fall at the Battle of the Somme, wearing the 2nd Foot Guards uniform, c. 1914. The Foot Guard Regiments were five formations from the Royal Prussian Army that although serving as Guards Corps, saw action as any other regiment.

1915 Franz Sinnen (1896-1916) di Jesteburg, perì nella battaglia della Somme, indossando l'uniforme della 2a guardia a piedi, c. 1914. I Reggimenti della Guardia a Piedi erano cinque formazioni dell'armata imperiale prussiana che, pur servendo come Guards Corps, erano mandati in prima linea come qualsiasi altro reggimento.

▼ **1916** German artillery NCO and soldiers standing near a Bavarian 24cm *"Ladungswerfer Erhardt"* trench mortar coupled on a railway. This kind of mortar's projectile was nicknamed by the British "rum jar", which eventually became obsolete by late in the war.

1916 Sottufficiale e soldati tedeschi di artiglieria bavarese vicino ad un mortaio da trincea "Ladungswerfer Erhardt" di 24 cm montato su binario. Questo tipo di proiettile di mortaio fu soprannominato "barattolo di rum", pezzo che divenne obsoleto alla fine della guerra.

1916 WAR IN THE GROUND, SEA AND AIR
1916 LA GUERRA IN TRINCEA, SUI MARI E NEI CIELI

◄ **1916 German driver August Simon** from the 2nd Replacement Department of the Driver-Battalions, 187th Division, standing with one of his comrades.

*1916 L'autista tedesco **August Simon** del 2 ° Reparto sostitutivo dei battaglioni guidatori, 187 ° divisione, in piedi in posa con uno dei suoi compagni.*

▼ **1916 Uboat crew**

1916 l'agguerrito equipaggio di un sottomarino tedesco.

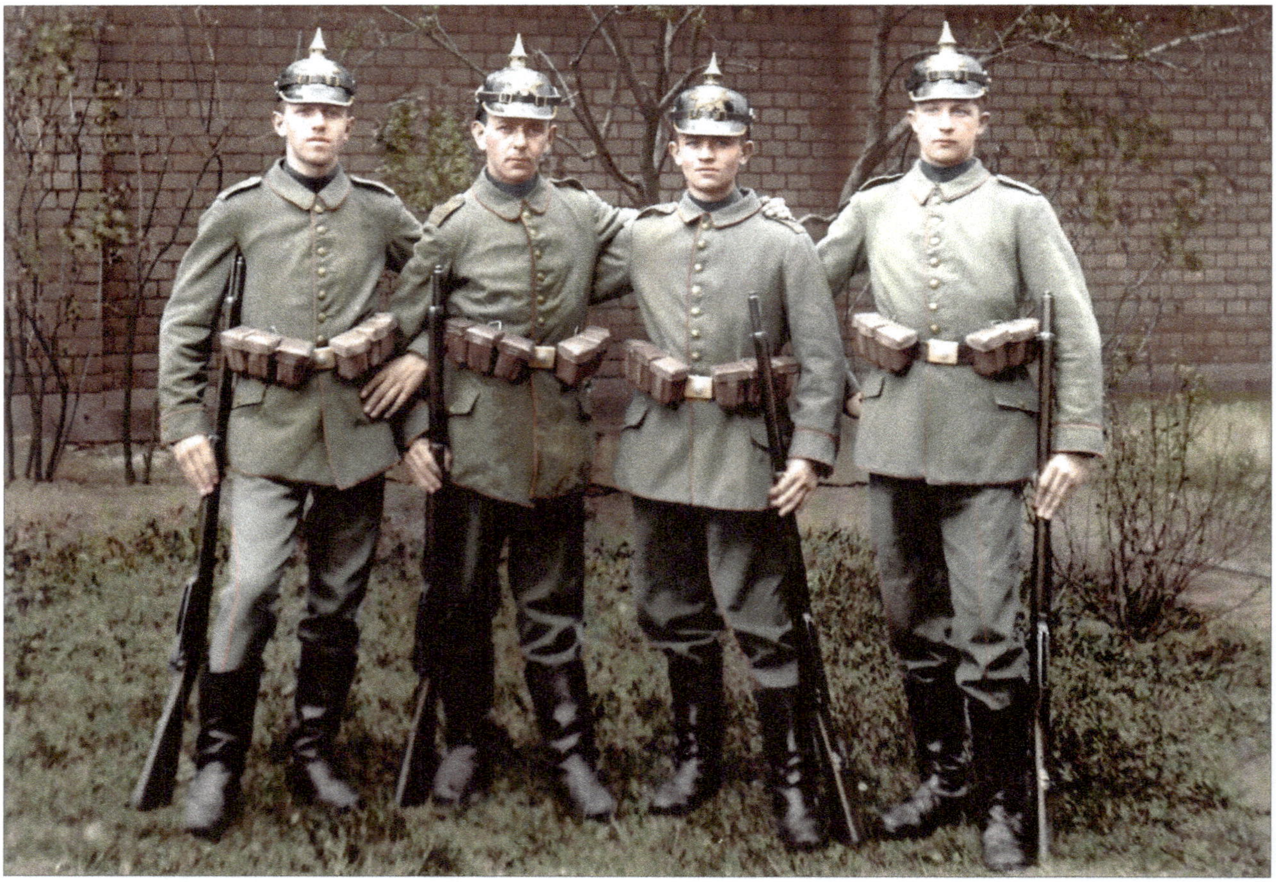

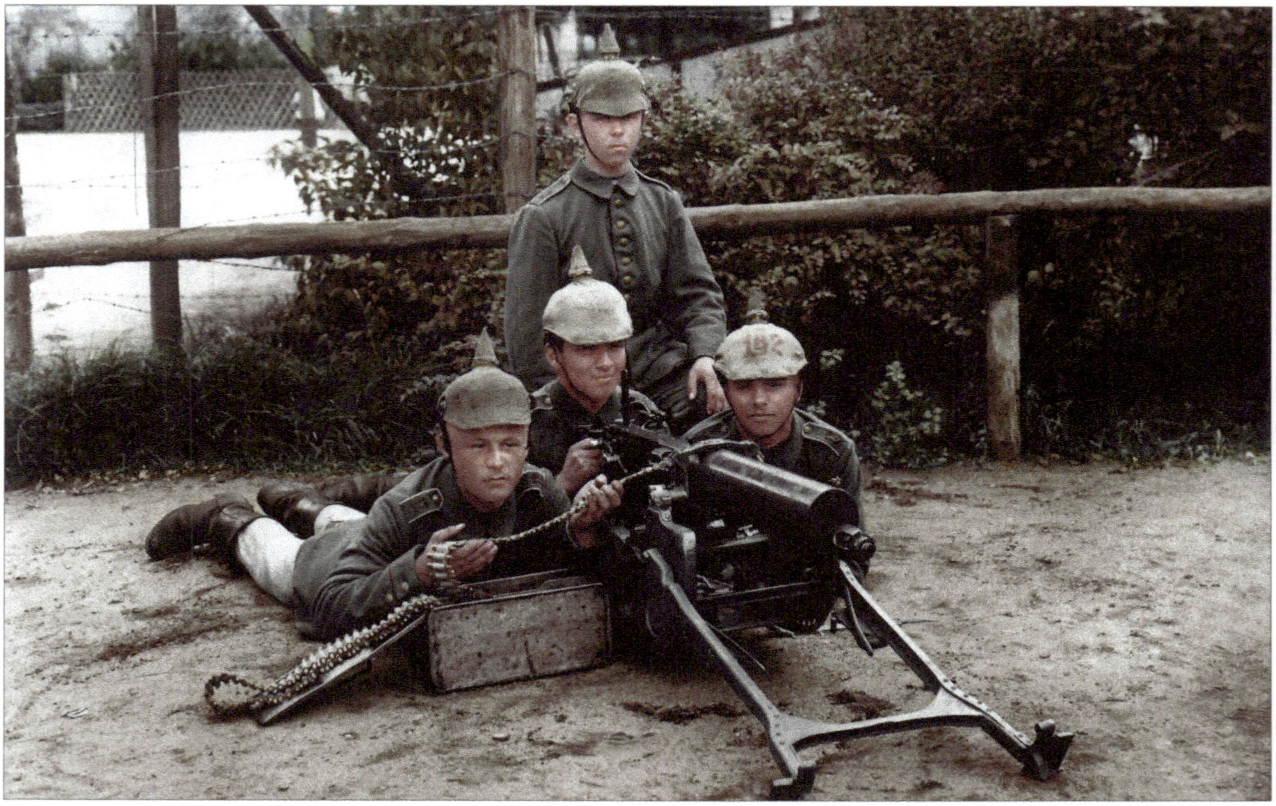

◄ **1916 Paul Klüge (1897-1916)**, on the left, with three of his comrades, wearing Pickelhaubes in Zittau, 21 April 1916. Six months later, Klüge would be missing and would never be seen again.

1916 Paul Klüge (1897-1916), a sinistra, con tre dei suoi compagni, tutti in pickelhaubes a Zittau, il 21 aprile 1916. Sei mesi dopo, Klüge fu ufficialmente dato per disperso e di lui non si seppe più nulla.

◄ **1916** Walter Klügel (1899-1964), a young butcher from Radeberg, on the right, with his MG 08 crew, 1916. They are wearing Pickelhaubes with the M1892 Überzug cover. With exposure to the sun, the Überzug eventually used to fade into a tan shade.

1916 Walter Klügel (1899-1964), un giovane macellaio di Radeberg, a destra, coi suoi camerati alla MG 08. Indossano Pickelhaubes con la copertura Überzug M1892.

▼ **1916** Two German soldiers and their mule wearing gas masks

1916 due soldati tedeschi ed il loro mulo; tutti con regolare maschera antigas

◄ **1916** Fritz Bauer from Kemnat, Swabia, proudly wearing his Wurttemberg Military Merit Medal shortly before returning to the battlefield.

1916 Fritz Bauer tedsco di Kemnat nella Svevia con indosso la medaglia per il merito del Württemberg.

▼ **1917** German cavalry officer from the Army of Württemberg, wearing an Iron Corss, fondles his dog after a horse ride near a railway, Northern France, c. 1917.

1917 Ufficiale di cavalleria del Württemberg, decorato con croce di ferro mentre accarezza il suo cane dopo una galoppata lungo il binario ferroviario. Nord della Francia.

☞ Next pages: **1917** A German Ehrhardt-Rheinmetall K-Flak anti-aircraft gun, between Flanders and Artois, 1917. The artefact on the far right is a rangefinder, a device that measures distance from the observer to the target.

1917 Un cannone tedesco antiaereo (Ehrhardt-Rheinmetall) situato fra le Fiandre e l'Artois. Notare il visore moderno per controllare la distanza di tiro.

IN THE IMMEDIATE BACK AREAS
NELLE IMMEDIATE RETROVIE

◀ **1917** Four German soldiers in bunk beds woken up for a surprise photograph. Among the many items that can be seen, there are gas mask canisters and trench flashlights. German trench defences, in contrast to British ones, had full underground rooms to accommodate the troops.

1917 Quattro fati tedeschi nella loro camerata colti di sorpresa dall'obiettivo fotografico. A differenza delle trincee inglesi, quelle tedesche erano molto ben organizzate.

▼ **1917** Members of a Train-Bataillon, responsible for transport and supply, with a self-constructed sham cannon imitating a Big Bertha, 1917.

1917 Soldati di un battaglione Treno alle prese con un finto cannone Berha

☞ Next pages: **1917** The Dog Hospital of the Messenger Dogs School, with German soldiers taking care of wounded dogs, c. 1917. 40,000 dogs, many of them recruited from homes of civilians, were trained and fought among other German soldiers on the battlefield.

1917 Ospedale tedesco per cani! Nel corso del conflitto i tedeschi usarono circa 40.000 cani in battaglia.

WW1 BORN THE TANKS
NASCONO I PRIMI CARRI ARMATI

◄ ▼ **1917** An unequipped Bavarian soldier, Nicolas Hiessler (1884-1952) posing in front of a destroyed British camouflaged Mark IV 'Female' tank, near Arras, 1917. 'Female' tanks, in opposition to 'Male' tanks, were tank versions carrying multiple machine guns instead of cannons.

1917 Il soldato bavarese Nicolas Hiessler (1884-1952) insieme al suo plotone, posa in fronte ad un carro armato inglese modello Mark IV (Femmina) distrutto vicino ad Arras.
I carri femmina, a differenza dei carri maschio avevano in dotazione diverse mitragliatrici invece dei cannoni.

◄ **Young German *Stoßtruppen*** (Schock trooper) during the Battle of the Somme, late 1916.

1916 Giovane recluta degli Sturmtruppen durante la battaglia delle Somme

◄ **1917** German artillery squad moving a 17 cm mittlerer *Minenwerfer* into position, Champagne, France, c. 1917. Germany developed a short-barrelled mortar called the *Minenwerfer*, built in three sizes, which lead to many advantages in trench warfare.

1917 Plotone di artiglieri tedeschi piazzano un pezzo da 17 (Minenwerfer) nella zona della Champagne in Francia

▼ **1918** A devastated battlefield with only one standing camouflaged artillery piece. During WWI, a new battle landmark was originated: mud and soil flying in the air and trees ripped to shreds could be seen due to artillery barrages.

1918 La devastazione del campo di battaglia con un solo pezzo artiglieria mimetizzato

☞ Next pages: **1917** Two machine gun operators and their NCO in a trench position, Belgium, 1917. The Stahlhelm and the MG08/15 probe the modernisation of the German Army, which started in the 1916, changing from Pickelhaubes to modern steel helmets.

1917 Una squadra di mitraglieri con la loro MG08/15 confermano la grossa modernizzazione dell'armata tedesca, iniziata nel 1916 con l'adozione dell'elmetto d'acciaio in luogo del Pickelhaube.

◄ **1916** Swabian cavalry NCO Wilhelm Müller from Ruit, present day Ostfildern, with wife and child, c. 1916. As it can be appreciated on his sword, he was a Unteroffiziermit Portepee (*NCO with sword knot*), a senior enlisted NCO entitled to wear a sword knot on his sabre.

1916 Wilhelm Müller Sottufficiale di cavalleria svevo di Ruit, fotografato con moglie e figlia.

▼ **1918** Artillery officers and NCOs posing in front of a destroyed bunker, blown up due to a shell barrage, c. 1918. The jackets they are wearing look like 'Kleiner Rock', a kind of uniform with two characteristic rows of buttons used mainly by officers.

1918 Soldati d'artiglieria in posa di fronte ad un bunker distrutto

☞ Next pages: **1917** The hairdresser Albert Schwanz and other soldiers of Seebataillone in the defensive trenches of the beaches of Oostende, 1917. Seebataillone (Sea battalion) were certain German troops of naval infantry or marines, counting with 70,000 men in 1918.

1917 Il barbiere Albert Schwanz e altri commilitoni di un SeeBattalione in una trincea vicino alla spiaggia di Ostenda. I battaglioni di mare, un misto di fanteria di marina arrivarono a contare 70.000 uomini nel 1918.

◄ **1917** Wilhelm Sinnen (1899-1968) from the 76th Infantry Regiment, in a photo studio of the occupied Belgium, c. 1917. He is wearing the plane M15 tunic, which replaced the M1910/14 tunic in 1915.

1917 Wilhelm Sinnen (1899-1968) del 76° Reggimento di fanteria, ritratto in una foto studio fatta in Belgio. Indossa la tunica M15 che rimpiazzò il modello M1910/14 nel 1915.

▼ **1918** German soldiers with camouflage helmets help wounded Belgian troops, Belgium. Two events turned worldwide opinion against Germany, which would be seen as an aggressor in Europe: the sinking of the RMS Lusitania and the Rape of Belgium, a series of war crimes that involved the assassination of 23,700 Belgian civilians.

1918 Soldati tedeschi con elemetti mimetici, aiutano due feriti belgi. Due furono gli eventi che fecero fare la parte dell'aggressore alla germania: L'affondamento del Lusitania e l'aggressione al neutrale Belgio.

◄ **1917** Soldier resting on the front while a rat curiously eats a loaf of beard resting aside his gear. Trench conditions provoked the spread of rats and lice, and with them came several diseases, such as the "trench fever". Also notice the complete German equipment.

1917 soldato tedesco che sfinito si lasci dormire nella sua trincea.

◄ **1915** Richard Bochalli (1848-1922) in Prussian uniform after being reactivated at the age of 67 to set up and run 3 prison camps in northern Germany. Noticeable decorations are, from left to right, the Iron Cross, the Order of the Red Eagle, the Order of the Crown, the Prussian Twelve Years Army Service Medal, the War Commemorative Medal of 1870/71, and the Centenary Medal.

1915 L'ufficiale tedesco Richard Bochalli insignito di numerose decorazioni al merito

▼ **1918** Nurses and injured soldiers peeling potatoes in front of a hospital in Cologne, c. 1915. Peeling potatoes is one of the most iconic images related to old warfare, since armies saw potatoes as a basic and cheap element for the soldier's diet.

1918 Nurse e soldati intenti a pelare patate. Nel 1918 la crisi alimentare negli imperi centrali si fece assai grave.

☞ Next pages: **1914** Prussian soldier shaves his officers in front of a well-fortified light bunker, during the so-called morning shave. Shaving was a daily routine for all troops during the Great War and something strictly required, and many times officially regulated.

1914 Un soldato semplice "fa la barba" ad un suo ufficiale all'interno di un fortino ben atrezzato nella linea delle trincee tedesche.

THE FRENCH

I FRANCESI

▲ French soldiers of the Infantry Regiment eat soup during the battle of the Aisne. Rare color photograph made with an Autochrome Lumière technique.

Soldati di fanteria francese in una rara foto fatta con la tecnica Autochrome Lumière

◄ 1914 "L'Alsace a la France.."
1914 Allegoria francese inneggiante alla rivincita da prendersi in Alsazia e Lorena.

1914 THE ETERNAL WAR ON GERMAN
LA LOTTA INFINITA FRA FRANCESI E TEDESCHI

◄ **1914 Mort pour la France** Auguste Peix (1894-1915) from the 157th Infantry Regiment, on a camp near the Alps, November 1914. The uniform and cap are the traditional ones used by the *Chasseurs Alpins* (Alpine Hunters). The bayonet is the "Rosalie".

1914 Auguste Peix (1894-1915) del 157° reggimento di fanteria. L'uniforme lo distingue come cacciatore alpino. Porta la baionetta denominata "Rosalie"

▼ **1914** Five French conscripts, some of them with their military papers stuck in their caps, before leaving the front, 1914. 3 million men were mobilized in August 1914, undertaking three years of obligatory service for all reservists of ages 24 to 30 who had completed their period of full-time service, and men up to the age of 45.

1914 Cinque coscritti francesi che secondo tradizione portano il foglio militare sopra il capo. Nell'agosto del 1914 ben 3 milioni di francesi vennero mobilitati. La leva era obbligatoria per la fascia di età che andava da 24-30 fino a 45 anni massimo.

◄ **1914** *le pantalon rouge c'est la France*. the uniforms with which France began the war were an heritage of the XIX century

1917 Stampa allegorica Dei primi mesi di Guerra, in cui non si è ancora manifestata l'immane tragedia che questi soldati saranno costretti a vivere Nei cinque anni successivi. L'uniforme Dei primi tempi era un'eredità del secolo precedente, lunga tunica blue e pantaloni Rossi.

▼ Six soldiers from the 86th Infantry Regiment in the Camp of La Courtine, 1914. The men are wearing delayed uniforms, such as the early "garance" coloured M1897 trousers.

Sei soldati dell'86° reggimento al campo di La Courtine. Gli uopmini indossano il vecchio pantalone color garance modello 1897.

◄ **1914** This chromophotography showing well the uniform and equipment of the French soldier at the beginning of the war.

1914 Altra cromofotografia che mostra bene l'uniforme e l'equipaggiamento del soldato francese a inizio guerra.

▼ **1915** Albert Joseph Pinaroli (1878-1945) from the 108th Territorial Infantry Regiment, left from the first row, with his comrades and a fellow dog on a trench. Territorial regiments were regiments made up of men aged 34 to 39, born between 1875 and 1880, who could not take first line combat.

1915 Il soldato Albert Joseph Pinaroli coi suoi camerati del 108° reggimento fanteria territoriale con la lor mascotte canina. I territoriali dovevano avere un'età compresa fra i 34 e i 39 anni.

☞ Next pages: **1916** Raymond Monteau and his comrades from the 7th Infantry Regiment in a searchlight automobile. Searchlights were used to create "artificial moonlights" to enhance opportunities for night attacks and to locate enemy aircraft.

1916 Raymond Monteau e i suoi camerati del 7° reggimento di fanteria Su una automobile-faro. Queste strutture di illuminazione servivano per creare quella luminosità lunare che doveva aiutare negli assalti notturni o a localizzare aerei nemici.

THE GREAT WAR IN THE TRENCHES
LA GUERRA E LE TRINCEE

◄ **1915 French soldiers using a periscope inside a trench.** The "French are cowards concerning military and always surrender" myth was not originated in WWI, as some may believe, but inevitably after the German invasion of 1940 and the later instalment of the puppet state of Vichy.

1916 Soldati francesi in trincea ispezionano le linee nemiche attraverso un periscopio

▼ **1916** Men from the 3rd Piece, 7th Battery, 39th Artillery Regiment posing in front of a *Canon de 75 1912 Schneider* (French 75 mm field gun), 1st August 1916, Battle of the Somme. Artillery units quickly adapted the M15 'blue horizon' uniform, and a special Adrian helmet, but quickly many non-official variations were born, with artillery men wearing custom white or beige corduroy shirts.

1916 Artiglieri del 39° Reggimento con un cannone da 75 mod. 1912. Battaglia delle Somme.

☞ Next pages: **1916** Captain Charles A. A. Noirtin from the 3rd Company, 4th Batallion, Morrocan Colonial Regiment being awarded the Croix de Guerre posthumously to his 9 years-old son Jean, surrounded by officers, Cherbourg, 28 January 1916. Captain Noirtin had died during the French offensive on Mametz, Somme, the 21st December 1914.

1916 Cerimonia per l'assegnazione della Croce di Guerra a giovane figlio (nove anni) del capitano Noirtin perito nell'offensiva di mametz, nelle Somme il 21 dicembre 1914.

◄ **1915** A French soldier, working as a cook, preparing a meal for the garrison while smoking a pipe near Rouen, c. 1915. M1877 2-liter canteens can be seen hanging on the left side.

1915 Un soldato, cuoco improvvisato prepara il rancio per la guarnigione fumando serenamente la sua pipa vicino a Rouen.

▼ **1916** François Camus, with a Croix de Guerre, playing cards with an NCO and a fellow soldier belonging to the 67th Brigade, 209th Regiment, a year after his unit had been dissolved, 1918. Camus was a farmer and, like many others, didn't know how to read.

1916 François Camus con la croce di Guerra mentre gioca a carte coi suoi camerati del 209° Reg.

☞ Next pages: **1916** Four 257th Infantry Regiment officers in the forest of Sainte-Marie, Bezange, January 1916. They are wearing TN gas masks, Coutrot Daggers No. 1, M1892 Revolvers, and a PA Ruby Gun.

1916 Quattro ufficiali del 257° Reggimento in tenuta mimietica con maschere antigas nella foresta di Sainte-Marie, Bezange.

◄ **1915** Group of soldiers from different regiments, Jean Charles Edouard Lafitte in the middle, in military uniform with kepi. The most interesting facts are Edouard's *Couvre-Képi* or Kepi Cover, an impermeable cover for the Kepi cap, along the M. 1877 dark blue overcoats.

1915. Gruppo di soldati di vari reggimenti riuniti per lo "scatto" fotografico

▼ **1915** French soldier from the 1st Battalion, 208th Infantry Regiment, 2nd Infantry Division, awarded with the Croix de Guerre, also wearing a black armband, which meant a close relative of him had died, c. 1918. He is wearing a *calot* (side cap) and a M1915 field uniform, which was introduced in 1915 to replace the former dark blue tunics.

1915 Soldato del 208° Reggimento con croce di ferro e banda a lutto portata per la morte di un parente.

▼ **1916** Philippe Pétain, 25 February 1916. Marshal Pétain was praised as a hero of war until 1940, when he became Chief of State of Vichy France, Nazi Germany's puppet state in Southern France.

1916 Philippe Pétain, fu considerato un eroe durante la prima Guerra mondiale, rovinerà poi la sua reputazione durante la seconda Guerra mondiale, offrendo la sua immagine alla Francia di Vichy

MUD, DUST AND BOMBS
FANGO, POLVERE E BOMBE

◄ **1915** Soldiers from the 3rd Artillery Regiment showing a shell with *Noél des Bosches 1915* ("Boches' Christmas 1915") inscribed, December 1915. Boche was a pejorative name referred to the Germans by the Allies, derived from *caboche* ("head" or "cabbage").

1915 Soldati del 3° reggimento ariglieria mostrano un proiettile con la scritta: "il natale dei tedeschi 1915" la parola boche derivava da "caboche" (testa dura).

▼ **1916** Louis Fretaux with his four best friends in the trenches of Verdun. Fretaux enlisted in the medical service, since his anti-war ideals prevented them to hold a rifle. He was one of the many soldiers who fought almost the entire war, enlisting the 2nd August 1914, having to leave the front the 16th October 1918 after being wounded during a German bombing.

1916 Louis Fretaux coi suoi migliori amici nella trincea di Verdun. Appartenente al copro medico, contrario per idealismo a portare un fucile negli anni prima della guerra, finirà per combattere il conflitto fino alla fine nel 1918.

BLEU HORIZON

L'AZZURRO FRANCESE

◄ **1917** Louis "*la pomme*" Paumier from the 403rd Infantry Regiment in Reims. His Adrian helmet and bayonet can be seen on the left side. The M15 Adrian helmet was the first standard helmet of the French Army after heavy shrapnel casualties prior to 1915, making it the first modern steel helmet.

1917 Luigi paumier (la mela)del 403° reggimento di fanteria fotografato a Reims in completo bleu Horizon..

▼ **1916** Medic and infantry soldiers in the trenches of Verdun. The Battle of Verdun, in which trenches played a major role, was fought from 21 February to 18 December 1916, and was the longest battle on the Western Front, taking 300,000 lives and leaving thousands injured.

1916 Ufficiale medico e infermieri in una trincea a Verdun. Combattuta fra il 21 febbraio e il 18 dicembre 1916, la battaglia di Verdun fu la più lunga della guerra e si prese la vita di oltre 300.000 soldati.

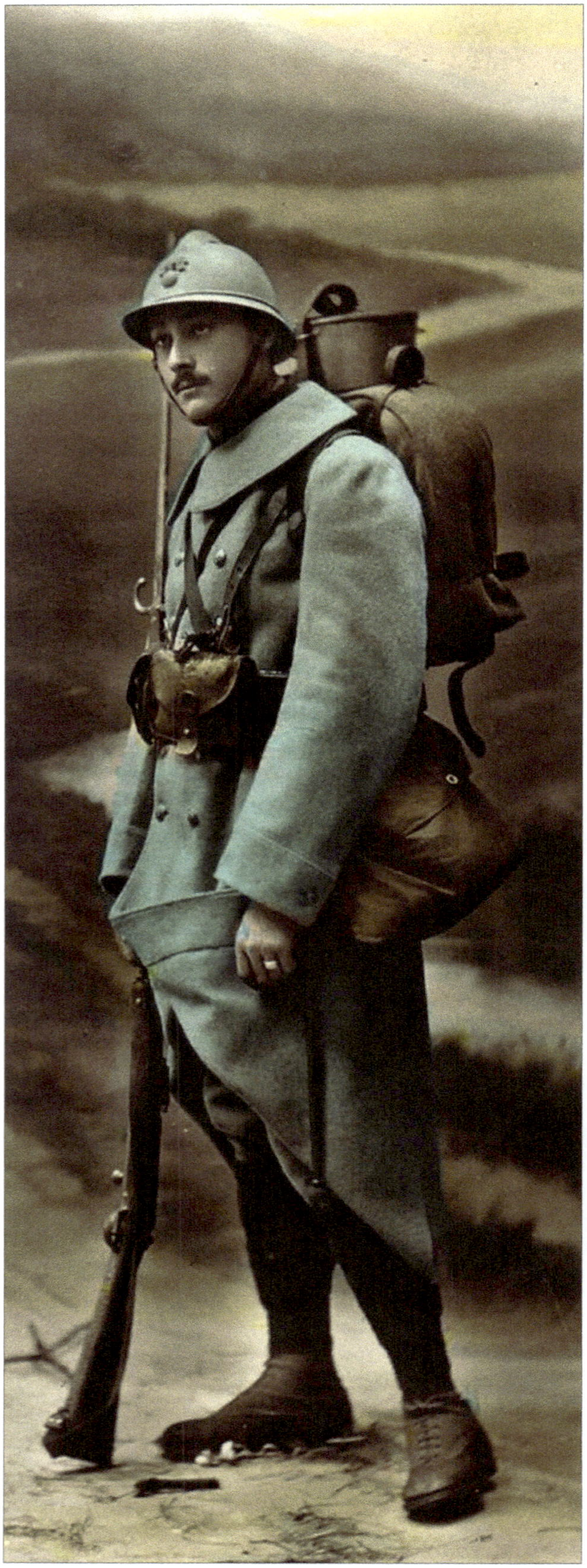

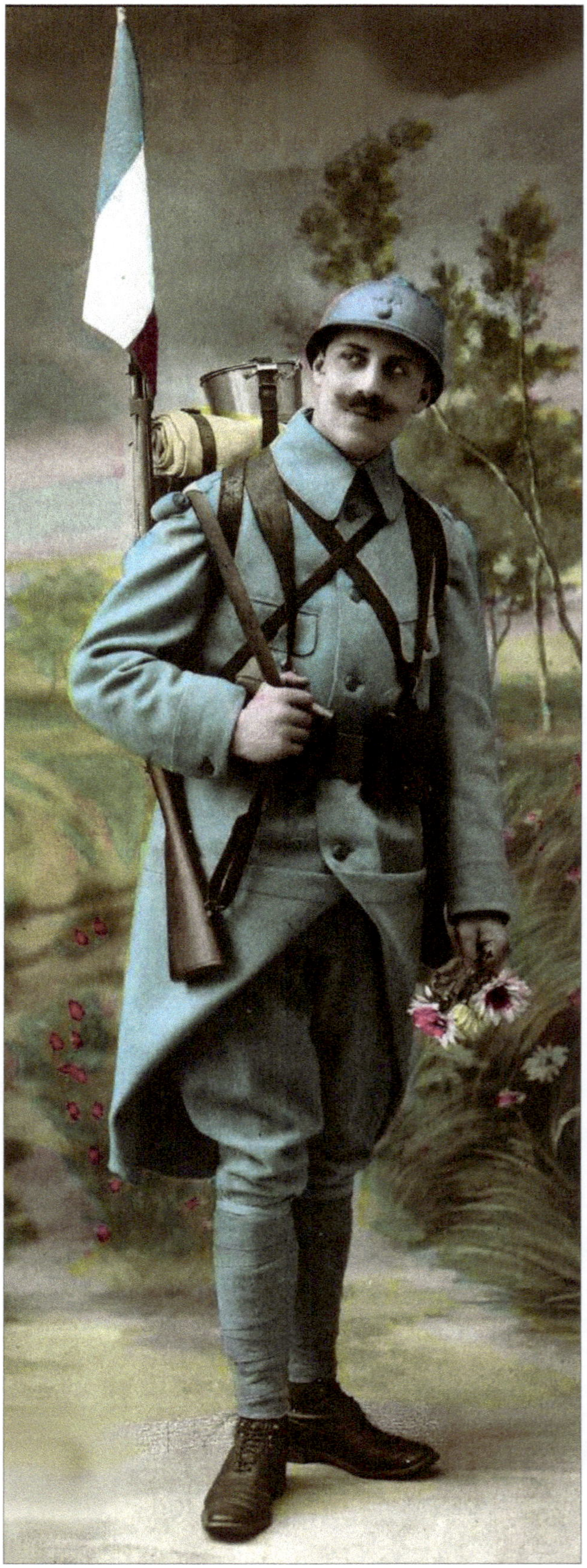

◄ **1917** The new French uniform consists of the light blue (Bleu horizon) and Adrian helmet.

1917 La nuova uniforme francese costituita dalla tenuta azzurro chiaro ed elmetto Adrian

▼ **1917** Two soldiers from the 22nd Infantry Regiment coming out of a shelter with M2 gas masks, c. 1917. The French army was the first to employ gas in the war, using tear gas grenades in August 1914, with poor results.

1917 due soldati del 22° Reggimento di fanteria escono dalla loro trincea indossando una maschera antigas del modello M2, Pochi sanno che furono proprio i francesi ad usare per primi il gas già nell'agosto 1914 ma si trattava di un prodotto di scarsa efficacia.

☞ Next pages: **1918** French doctors and nurses, both wearing the French Red Cross Military Secours Medal, operating a patient with a complex surgical instrument, possibly magnetic to remove shell, near Sens. In World War I and its post-war period the paper of medicine played a major role for the first time in history, from operations *in situ* to later face reconstructions.

1918 Equipe medica intenta ad operare un povero soldato ferito.

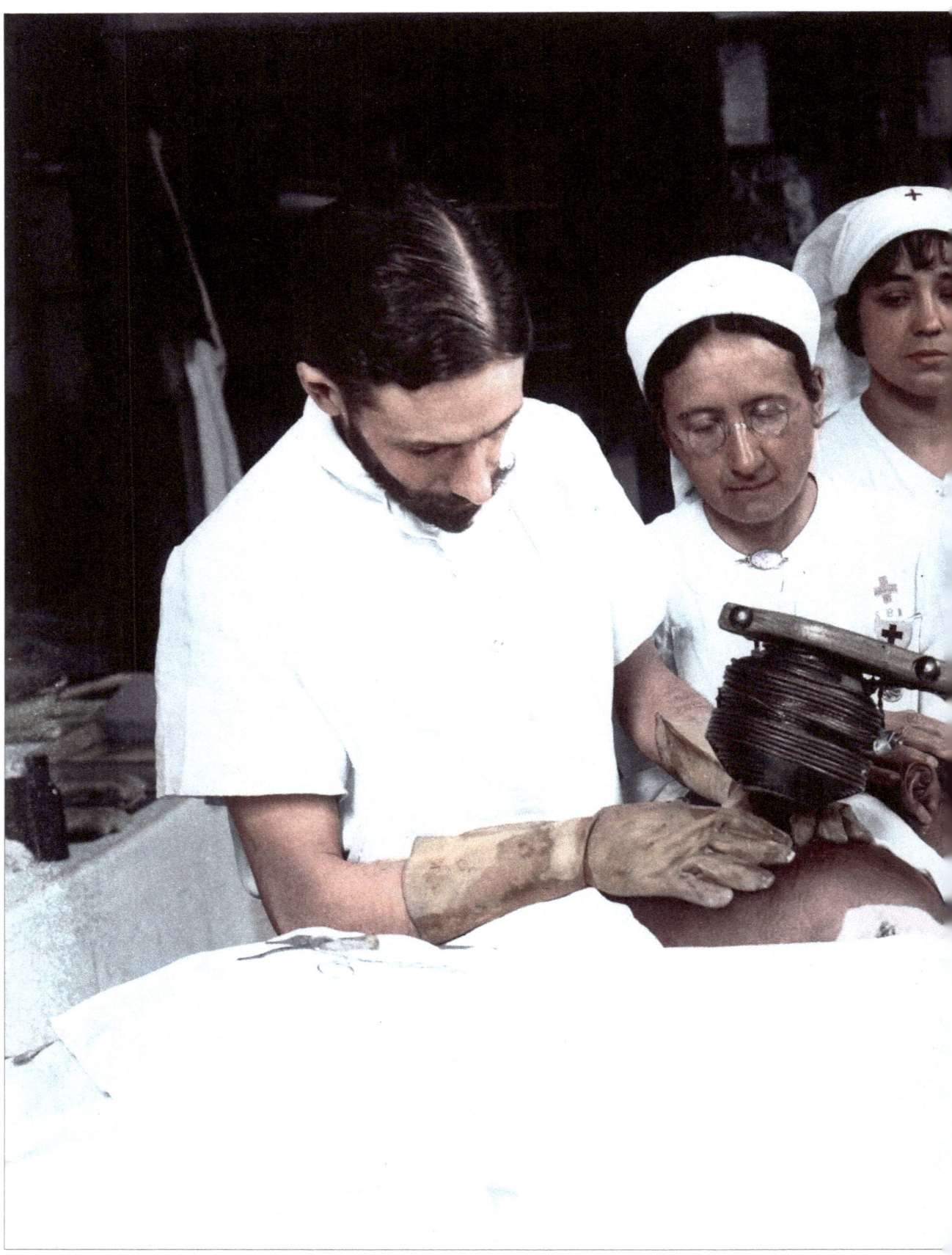

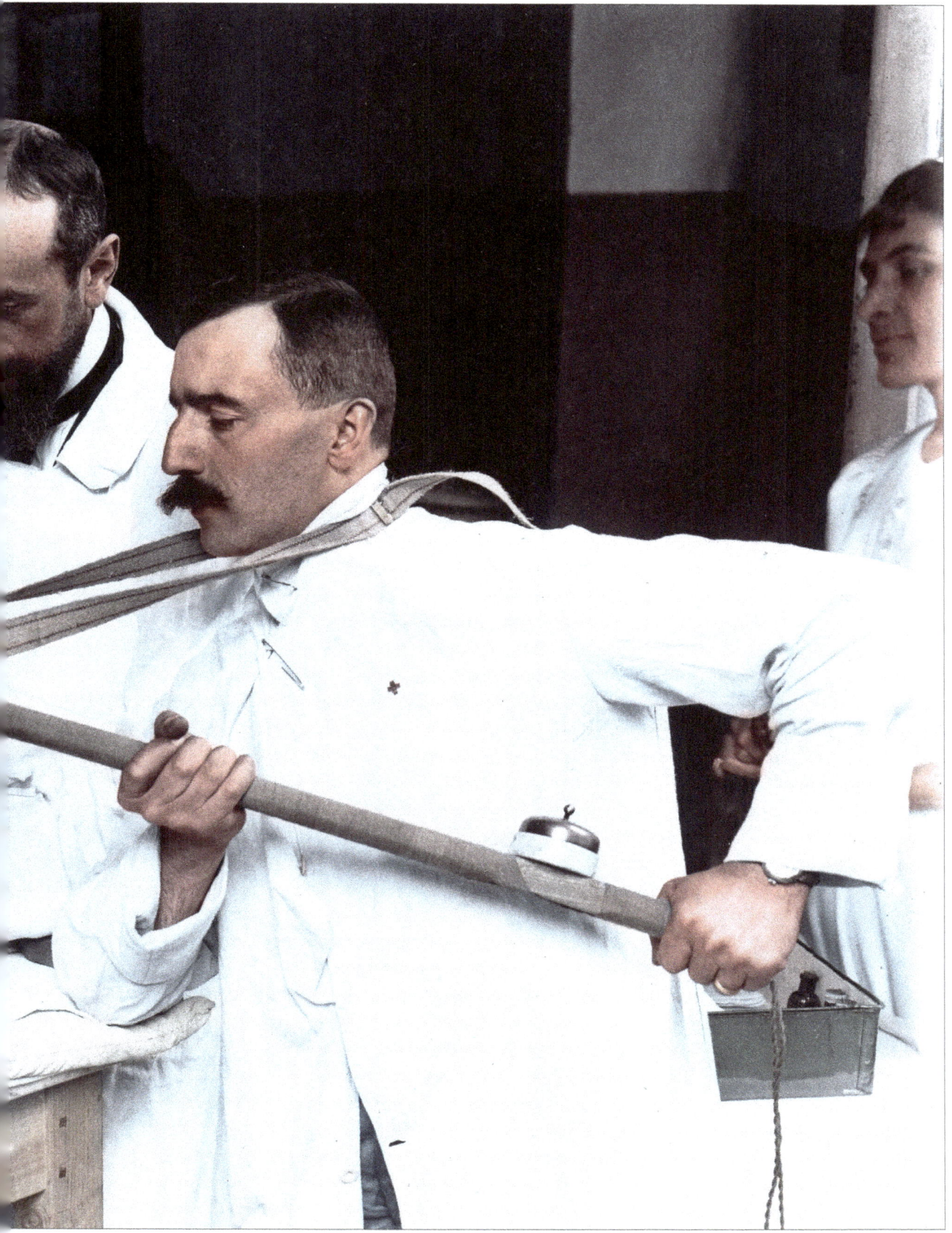

AIRPLANES & TANKS
CARRI ARMATI E AEREI

◄ **1916** French pilot Charles Nungesser with his mechanic Pochon from the (GC 12) 'Les Cigognes', in front of his 'The Knight of Death' Nieuport 17, Winter 1916. Nungesser (1892-1927) was one of the greatest French ace pilots, with 43 confirmed victories. After the war, Nungesser mysteriously disappeared on a transatlantic flight from Paris to New York.

1916 il famoso asso francese Charle Nungesser con il suo fidato meccanico Pochon accanto all'aereo biplano che reca il suo sinistro simbolo.

▼ **1917** Schneidr CA1 tank, the first French tank ever produced, from the 3rd Battery, in camouflage pattern, July 1917. At far left, French Morrocan 'Spahis' colonial soldiers, as well as a dog at the top can be seen. The Schneider CA1 was designed to open passages for the infantry through barbed wire and then to suppress German machine gun nests.

1917 Lo Scneider CA1 fu il primo carro armato francese mai prodotto, qui in versione mimetica.

☞ **1917** French pilot and photographer Justine Usse, with Air Wings and Croix de Guerre, in front of his Sopwith Camel 'Marcelle', c. 1917. The story of Usse is very similar to the average WWI pilot career: he first enlisted as an infantryman, was wounded after a mine explosion and, unable to return into the battlefield, was drafted into the aviation after 25 hours of flight.

1917 Il pilota francese Justine Usse, decorato con croce di guerra, accanto al suo Sopwith camel chiamato "Marcel"

◄ **1917** Captain Charles Goulon (1888-1922) from the 315th Infantry Regiment wearing the Croix de Guerre ribbon on the trenches near Lorraine.

1917 Il capitano Charles Goulon (1882-1922) del 315° reggimento di fanteria decorato di croce di guerra nelle trincee della Lorena.

▼ **1917** Horse-drawn vehicles take a break at the Somme, 1917. A railway and a locomotive can be seen on the background as well as a Berliet CBA truck. Horses participated during World War One, especially in the early stages, and in wide numbers, serving many times in very severe conditions.

1917 Veicoli ippotrainati sulle Somme

◄ **1915** Senegalese soldier serving in French army who jokes bringing two German pikelhaube helmets on his head.

1915 Soldato senegalese al servizio francese che ironizza portando in testa ben due elmi pikelhaube tedeschi.

▼ **1917** Artillery soldier from the 269ᵗʰ Infantry Regiment warning of a gas attack. The use of gas, delivered many almost every belligerent throughout World War I, constituted a war crime, violating two Hague Conventions on Land Warfare, which prohibited the use of "poison or poisoned weapons" in warfare.

1917 Soldato d'artiglieria del 269° Reggimento da l'allarme per un imminente attacco di gas.

◄ **1918** Jacques Garnier, Inspector General in the Colonial Army, and later medical inspector in the Third Army, with his son Charles "Cat", c. 1918. Both served three consecutive years, according to the chevrons.

1918 Padre e figlio Garnier, due generazioni di comandanti francesi

▼ **1917** The flag of the 114th Infantry Regiment in Paris. Lumiere chromophotography.

1917 La bandiera del 114° Reggimento di Fanteria a parigi. Cromofotografia Lumiere.

☞ Next pages: **1918** Barber Camille Veyri haircutting his comrades from the 234th Infantry Regiment in Sermoise, 2 March 1918. During WWI, soldiers wore very short hair due to body lice. Although French soldiers were known as *Poilu* ("Hairy one"), they had to shave their beards frequently, so gas masks fit properly; moustaches, however, could be widely seen on the front.

1918 Ubn barbiere sistema i capelli a due suoi camerati del 234° reggimento di fanteria a Sermoise.

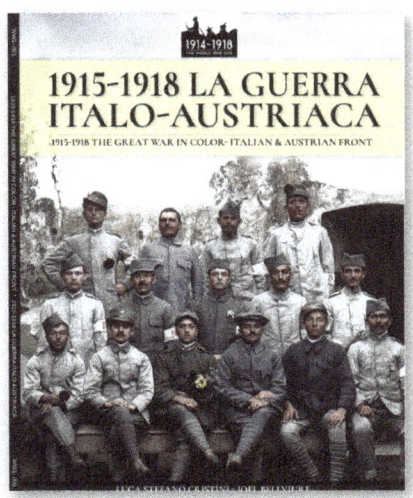

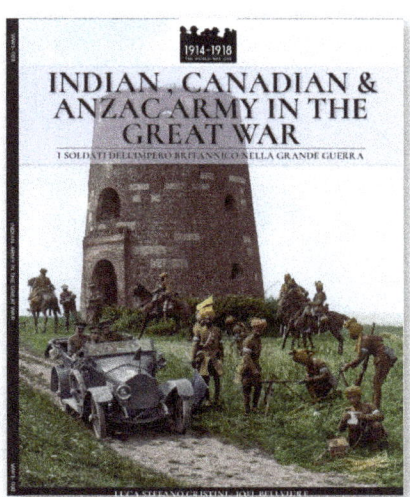

Books also in this series:

WW1-001 - 1915-1918 la Guerra Italo-Austriaca (The Great war in color -Italian & Austrian front)

WW1-002 - 1914-1918 German wartime propaganda

WW1-003 - 1915-1918 Italian pro & cons satire

WW1-004 - German & French Army in the Great War

WW1-005 - 1914-1918 French wartime satire

WW1-006 - Indian, Canadian & Anzac Army in the Great War

WW1-007 - English & US Army in the Great War

WW1-008 - Russian, Turkish and Balkan Army in the Great War

1914-1918
THE WORLD WAR ONE

SOLDIERSHOP PUBLISHING

BOOKS TO COLLECT